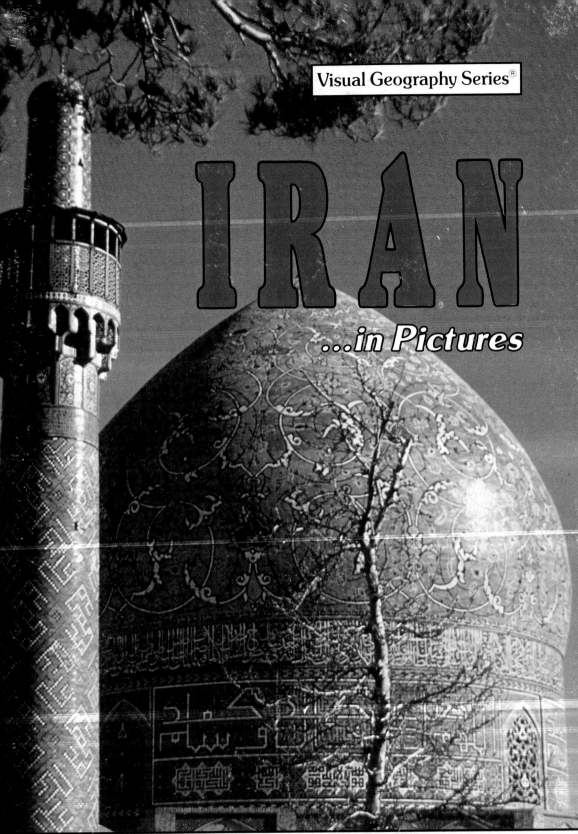

Visual Geography Series®

Prepared by
Geography Department

Lerner Publications Company
Minneapolis

IRAN
...in Pictures

Independent Picture Service

A lone truck makes its way across a desert area in Iran.

This is an all-new edition of the Visual Geography Series. Previous editions have been published by Sterling Publishing Company, New York City, and some of the original textual information has been retained. New photographs, maps, charts, captions, and updated information have been added. The text has been entirely reset in 10/12 Century Textbook.

LIBRARY OF CONGRESS CATALOGING-IN-PUBLICATION DATA

Iran in pictures.

(Visual geography series)
Includes index.
Summary: Iran's topography, history, society, economy, and government are concisely described, augmented by photographs, maps, charts, and captions.
1. Iran. [1. Iran] I. Lerner Publications Company. Geography Dept. II. Series: Visual geography series (Minneapolis, Minn.)
DS254.5.I744   1988   955   88-6818
ISBN 0-8225-1848-1 (lib. bdg.)

International Standard Book Number: 0-8225-1848-1
Library of Congress Catalog Card Number: 88-6818

VISUAL GEOGRAPHY SERIES®

Publisher
Harry Jonas Lerner
Associate Publisher
Nancy M. Campbell
Senior Editor
Mary M. Rodgers
Editor
Gretchen Bratvold
Assistant Editors
Dan Filbin
Kathleen S. Heidel
Illustrations Editor
Karen A. Sirvaitis
Consultants/Contributors
Isaac Eshel
Dr. Ruth F. Hale
Sandra K. Davis
Designer
Jim Simondet
Cartographer
Carol F. Barrett
Indexer
Kristine S. Schubert
Production Manager
Richard J. Hannah

Independent Picture Service

The city of Ahvaz is located 100 miles north of the Persian Gulf in the province of Khuzestan.

Acknowledgments

Title page photo courtesy of Minneapolis Public Library and Information Center.

Elevation contours adapted from *The Times Atlas of the World,* seventh comprehensive edition (New York: Times Books, 1985).

1 2 3 4 5 6 7 8 9 10 97 96 95 94 93 92 91 90 89 88

Unmindful of smoke escaping from a nearby cement factory, camels graze on a rocky hillside in Iran.

Contents

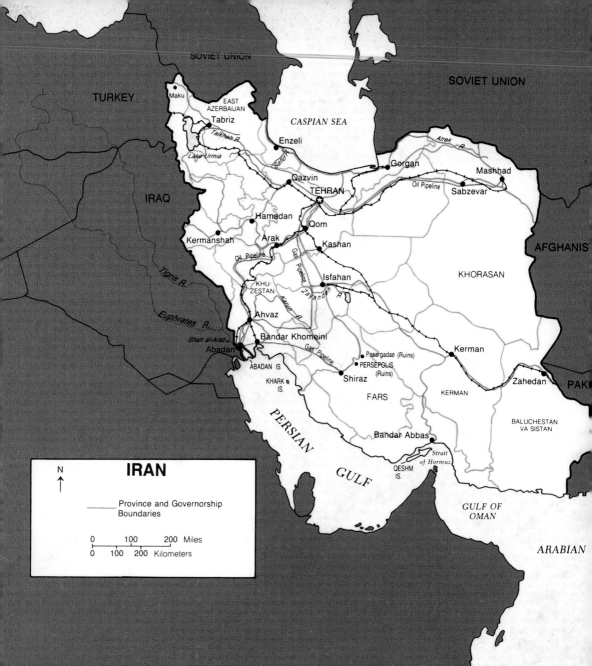

IRAN

SOVIET UNION

SOVIET UNION

TURKEY

Maku

EAST
AZERBAIJAN

Tabriz

CASPIAN SEA

Talkheh R.

Enzeli

Lake Urmia

Sefid R.

Qazvin

Gorgan

Atrek R.

Mashhad

Oil Pipeline

Sabzevar

IRAQ

TEHRAN

Hamadan

Qom

Kermanshah

Arak

Kashan

KHORASAN

Oil Pipeline

Gas Pipeline

Isfahan

AFGHANIS

Tigris R.

KHU-
ZESTAN

Karun R.

Zayandeh R.

Euphrates R.

Ahvaz

Shatt al-Arab

Bandar Khomeini

Gas Pipeline

Kerman

Abadan

Pasargadae (Ruins)

PERSEPOLIS
(Ruins)

ABADAN IS.

KHARK
IS.

Shiraz

KERMAN

Zahedan

PAK

FARS

BALUCHESTAN
VA SISTAN

PERSIAN

Bandar Abbas

Strait
of Hormuz

QESHM
IS.

GULF

GULF OF
OMAN

N

IRAN

ARABIAN

Province and Governorship
Boundaries

0   100   200 Miles

0   100   200 Kilometers

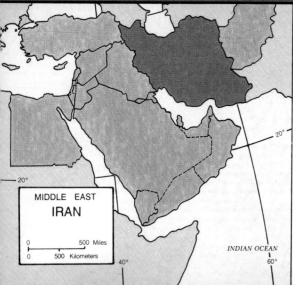

MIDDLE EAST
IRAN

20°

20°

20°

INDIAN OCEAN

40°

60°

0   500 Miles

0   500 Kilometers

METRIC CONVERSION CHART
To Find Approximate Equivalents

WHEN YOU KNOW:	MULTIPLY BY:	TO FIND:
AREA		
acres	0.41	hectares
square miles	2.59	square kilometers
CAPACITY		
gallons	3.79	liters
LENGTH		
feet	30.48	centimeters
yards	0.91	meters
miles	1.61	kilometers
MASS (weight)		
pounds	0.45	kilograms
tons	0.91	metric tons
VOLUME		
cubic yards	0.77	cubic meters
TEMPERATURE		
degrees Fahrenheit	0.56 (*after* subtracting 32)	degrees Celsius

The ruins of Persepolis—the capital of the ancient Persian Empire—lie near Shiraz in south central Iran. Founded by the Persian emperor Darius I (called the Great), Persepolis was the hub of a realm that stretched from India to Egypt.

Introduction

Iran, the name since 1935 of the country in the Middle East long referred to as Persia, is one of the world's oldest nations. The ancient Persians ruled an empire that stretched from the Indus River in India to the Nile River in Egypt. Over the centuries, this region became the prize of several conquerors—including the Greeks, the Parthians, the Sasanians, the Turks, and the Afghans.

Many ethnic groups, religions, and civilizations have left their imprint on the nation's culture. Despite these foreign influences, Iranians have had the strength not only to survive but also to absorb and adapt to outside elements while holding on to their own customs and traditions.

Although it has rich oil resources, Iran entered the twentieth century as an economically underdeveloped country. After Iranian oil production became a successful industry in the late 1940s, the Iranian government began a period of social and industrial change that brought its people needed reforms. Much of the profits, however, went to U.S.- or British-owned companies, and Iran's kings (called shahs) worked closely with the foreign groups.

5

Before his overthrow in 1979, Mohammad Reza Pahlavi, the former shah of Iran, had a great influence on world politics. He invested the nation's earnings from oil in many foreign firms, including the Krupp steelworks in Germany. Under the shah's guidance, government-owned Iranian banks loaned vast sums of money to nations throughout the world. Iran was one of the first members of OPEC, the Organization of Petroleum Exporting Countries, which influences oil prices and determines the amount of oil produced by OPEC members. The shah's plans also covered internal developments, such as building up Iran's armed forces and modernizing the city of Tehran into a major world capital.

Some of Iran's vast oil resources are tapped offshore through drilling platforms in the Persian Gulf.

Mohammad Reza Pahlavi (center), a former shah of Iran, talked with U.S. Army officers during joint military exercises in the 1970s.

Although Iran was on its way to Westernized development and self-sufficiency in the 1970s, internal unrest over the authoritarian royal government made the regime unstable. Clergy of the Islamic religion—the major faith in Iran—disagreed with the country's Western direction. After numerous antigovernment demonstrations, in which many Iranians were killed, the government placed the military in charge of keeping order.

A revolution in 1979 brought to power Ruhollah Khomeini, who is called an ayatollah (an important and learned religious leader). He had been in exile from Iran since 1964 for opposing the government's program of reform. The nation turned toward a more conservative style of government based on Islamic law, with Khomeini as its spiritual and political leader. Iran's sect of Islam—called Shiism—is

Soon after the shah was overthrown in 1979, Iranian students seized the U.S. embassy in Tehran, the capital of Iran. Here, demonstrators meet in support of the embassy seizure, which involved the two-year detainment of 52 U.S. hostages.

central to the goals and decisions of the Iranian government.

Iran is now trying to persuade other countries to accept its anti-Western, antimodern ideas. At the same time, the nation is attempting to regain its oil markets and to provide for its growing population. Iran must confront declining oil prices and increasing isolation from nearby Arab states. The nation's long-term stability will also depend on achieving a lasting peace with its neighbor Iraq after eight years of war.

A woman from a nomadic ethnic group wears a head and face covering adopted in accordance with the rules of the Koran (Islamic holy writings) as a sign of modesty.

A cargo ship of the Islamic Republic of Iran Shipping Lines steams through the waters of the Persian Gulf, which forms the nation's southern territorial boundary.

1) The Land

Situated in southwestern Asia with an area of 636,296 square miles, the Islamic Republic of Iran is more than twice the size of Texas and shares boundaries with five nations. The Soviet Union, separated into two sections by the Caspian Sea, lies to the north. Iraq and Turkey flank Iran to the west, and Pakistan and Afghanistan form the country's eastern border.

The nation's southern boundary lies along the Persian Gulf and the Gulf of Oman, which leads to the Arabian Sea.

Among several islands that Iran has claimed as part of its territory is Qeshm, which is located in the Strait of Hormuz. The strait is a narrow channel that connects the Persian Gulf with the Gulf of Oman.

Topography

Iran is a land of many contrasts. Snow-capped mountains, ranging in height from 6,000 to 12,000 feet, enclose a rocky central plateau and arid salt deserts that support almost no life. A northern coastal strip along the Caspian Sea is the most fertile and most heavily populated region of the country. Along a section of the Persian Gulf lies Iran's rich bed of petroleum deposits, called the Khuzestan Plain.

Iran occupies the western and larger half of the great Plateau of Iran, a level region that links the steppes (semi-arid grasslands) of central Asia to the plateau of Asia Minor (mainland Turkey). Scientists also view the plateau as part of a larger topographical feature that extends east into Afghanistan and Pakistan. Underground plates of land have folded and pressed the edges of the landscape, forming several mountain ranges. As a result, Iran's topography has frequent fault lines, or seams, that move as pressure builds up beneath the earth. These movements often create devastating earthquakes.

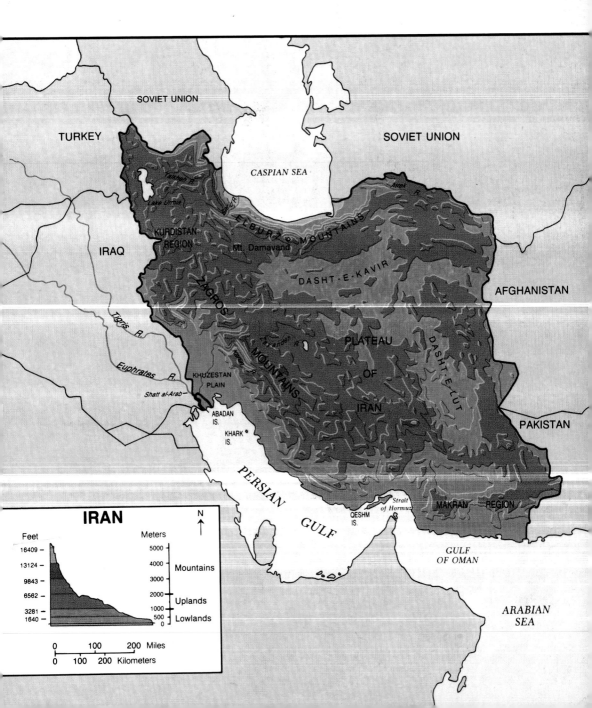

Iran's section of the plateau is triangular and is bounded by mountain chains. The Zagros Mountains lie in the west, and streams cut deep, narrow gorges through this range, carrying water to fertile valleys in the region. Much of the area is very rugged and is populated mostly by nomadic (seasonally wandering) peoples.

The Elburz range is located in the north and contains Mount Damavand (18,934 feet), the highest peak in the nation. These mountains are made of volcanic rock and rise above a 70-mile-wide coastal strip along the southern shore of the Caspian Sea—the world's largest landlocked body of water. The mountains drop sharply from 10,000 feet to the marshy water's edge. The fertile coast was actually a section of the sea floor, which was uncovered by the slow shrinking of the Caspian Sea. The coastal landscape is generally regular, with a few small lagoons that provide sheltered places for boats to anchor.

In the center of the Plateau of Iran is a great desert region that once formed the bed of a lake. The two salt deserts on the plateau comprise about 25 percent of Iran's total land area. Some forms of life grow in the Dasht-e-Kavir to the north, where the soil is less salty and where oases

Shepherds lead their flock to pasture through the rugged terrain of one of Iran's mountain ranges.

In desert areas of eastern Iran, soil cracks from lack of water and from the relentless pressure of the hot, dry climate.

Some species of Iran's birds live along the shores of the Caspian Sea, which borders hundreds of miles of the nation's territory.

(fertile areas) exist. But few explorers have ever dared to venture into the hostile wasteland of the Dasht-e-Lut to the south.

At the northern end of the Persian Gulf, within Khuzestan province, lies the plain that contains most of Iran's oil deposits. Tapped since 1908, the petroleum fields are clustered near Iran's eastern border with Iraq.

Bodies of Water

Water has always been a vital need on the Plateau of Iran. The few streams flowing into it often disappear into salt marshes. Three large rivers flow outward from the mountains, two of which, the Atrek and the Safid, enter the Caspian Sea. The other one—the Karun—is the only river in Iran that is navigable. It travels from the Zagros Mountains to the Shatt al-Arab—a narrow channel that marks the joining of the Tigris and Euphrates rivers—and then flows into the Persian Gulf.

The great variation of water volume in Iran's rivers poses a major problem for the country's inhabitants. Streams fill with raging waters from rains and melted snow

Two workers remove earth from a new *kanat*, or well, that contains an underground water supply for irrigation.

Portage animals and their owner cross a wooden bridge that spans one of Iran's swiftly moving mountain streams.

in the spring, only to become totally dry by late summer. Water remains underground, however, and Iranians have tapped groundwater supplies for irrigation since ancient times. During the reign of Mohammad Reza Pahlavi, several large dams were built in the country to reduce flooding, to conserve water, and to generate electricity.

Other than the Caspian Sea, Iran has few inland bodies of water. Most result from seasonal rains and dry up in the summertime. Indeed, the Caspian Sea loses more water from evaporation than it receives from streams feeding into it. The country's largest body of water lying completely within Iran is Lake Urmia in the northwest, near Tabriz.

Climate

Like its topography, Iran's climate also has some extreme contrasts. In general,

Lake Urmia lies between Iran's northwestern provinces of West and East Azerbaijan.

however, the climate of the northern and eastern parts is more moderate than the southern and western regions. Nevertheless, Tehran, in northern Iran, has summer temperatures as high as 118° F during the day.

13

Courtesy of FAO

The Iranian government has planted drought-resistant vegetation in an attempt to prevent soil erosion in a sandy area near the Dasht-e-Kavir.

Winter, especially from mid-December to mid-February, is severely cold, with snow, ice, and below-zero temperatures. Iran's spring is short and often rainy; autumn is long, with sunny days and cool nights.

Tehran receives about 15 inches of precipitation annually and is considered semi-arid. The region north of Tehran, toward the Elburz Mountains, receives more rain —the city of Qazvin, for example, gets about 22 inches annually. The Elburz range receives up to 30 inches, some of it in the form of snow.

The region with the most temperate year-round climate is the narrow, lush strip of land between the Elburz Mountains and the Caspian Sea. The beach was once known as the "Iranian Riviera" because its climate is similar to that of the luxurious resort area in France. The region near the Caspian Sea receives about 25 inches of rain, which falls throughout the year.

The area around the Persian Gulf is the hottest in Iran, and temperatures can rise to 140° F in summer. This factor, plus high humidity, makes life very hard for people on the islands of Abadan and Khark, both of which lie in the gulf. In the winter months, high temperatures in this region range between 70° F and 85° F, with cool evenings. Despite high humidity, rain is rare, and annual precipitation is between three and five inches.

The west, especially in the area that is close to Turkey, receives more rain and snow at the higher elevations. Lower elevations—close to the Iraqi border—are known for their hot climate.

Flora and Fauna

The northern part of Iran contains the last remaining thickly forested area of the Middle East. Over the years, this forest has deteriorated through overcutting, and a reforestation scheme has begun. Gorgan

Independent Picture Service

Kenaf, a coarse, weedlike plant, grows well in Iran and provides rough fibers used in the production of sacks and canvas material.

in northern Iran and Iranian Kurdistan in the northwest grow some of the world's finest walnut trees, whose lumber French furniture makers have been buying for the past 300 years. At the foot of the Elburz Mountains lies a region dotted with oak, willow, fig, and pomegranate trees. Orange, lemon, and date trees also grow there, as well as in other parts of the country. A species of plane tree shades the broad avenues of Tehran, and cypresses line the streets of Shiraz.

An important tree is the pistachio—prized for its nuts and also for its wood—which is widespread in the northern part of the country. In the south, date trees surround streams and oases. These trees are frequently seen along the border with Iraq and on the Shatt al-Arab. Scrub vegetation and cacti dominate the landscape of the arid central plateau.

The northern forests provide habitats for tigers, panthers, wolves, foxes, and bears. Rabbits, jackals, deer, and badgers are also fairly common. Inland and in the south live some of Iran's abundant birdlife, including pheasants, pelicans, partridges, and flamingos. Wild goats and sheep inhabit the southern mountains.

Courtesy of Embassy of the Islamic Republic of Iran, Ottawa

A view of the northern province of Mazandaran, which lies in the Elburz Mountains, reveals the lush forests that still thrive near the Caspian Sea.

The Caspian Sea and its inlets host many varieties of fish, such as sturgeon, whitefish, and herring.

Cities

About half of Iran's 50.3 million people live in urban areas. Many Iranians moved to the cities beginning in the mid-twentieth century, when large-scale urban modernization offered the promise of better jobs.

Tehran (population six million) lies in northern Iran at over 3,800 feet above sea level. The city is the nation's most important industrial and cultural hub, as well as being the largest urban area in the country. The capital of what is now Iran since 1795, the city underwent extensive modernization during the twentieth century. Skyscrapers and modern boulevards have been built near ancient mosques (Islamic houses of worship) and narrow, winding streets. Since the 1979 revolution, Tehran's economy has been disrupted, but the city's industrial sector still manufactures textiles, weapons, automobiles, and cement for use throughout the country.

In the nineteenth and twentieth centuries, Mashhad (population over one million) became of strategic importance because of its nearness to Russia and Afghanistan. But the city—which lies in the rich agricultural region of Khorasan province—had been a major trade center between India and Persia for centuries. In addition, the city has become a religious site for Shiite Muslims.

Iran's third largest city is Tabriz (population 900,000), the capital of Persia in the fifteenth century and now the main urban center of northwestern Iran. A junction for roads and railways, the city also lies on the

Courtesy of Minneapolis Public Library and Information Center

Extensively modernized in the twentieth century, Tehran has become the commercial and industrial hub of the nation.

Isfahan's fine Islamic architecture, such as this mosque (Islamic place of worship) built for a seventeenth-century shah, distinguishes the city from Iran's other urban centers.

A carving on one of the pillars at Persepolis depicts the Persian emperor Darius I fighting a mythological animal.

Talkheh River. Carpets, leather goods, soap, and dried fruits are among Tabriz's manufactured products. The city has suffered frequently from earthquake damage and foreign occupation.

In the sixteenth century, the Safavid shah Abbas I chose to rule his Persian lands from Isfahan (population 900,000), in west central Iran. The shah built several noteworthy mosques throughout his long reign, and Isfahan still enjoys the beauty of its traditional Islamic architecture. Industrial products made in Isfahan include textiles and steel.

Shiraz (population 800,000) is the commercial center of Fars province and produces cement, sugar, fertilizers, and carpets. The city also lies near the ruins of Persepolis—the capital of the ancient Persian Empire.

This detail from a golden bowl dates from the Achaemenid period, which lasted from the seventh to the fourth centuries B.C. The piece is engraved with a griffin, or winged lion, along with several other legendary creatures.

Courtesy of Dale O'Dell/*Aramco World*

2) History and Government

The earliest archaeological evidence of human beings in Iran dates from 100,000 years ago. Scientific studies show that people settled in the region about 15,000 years ago. The first recorded culture in Iran was organized by the Elamites, who may have lived in the southwest by about 3000 B.C.

The Medes and the Persians

At the beginning of the Iron Age (about 1000 B.C.), two Aryan peoples—the Medes and the Persians—wandered down through the Caucasus Mountains of central Asia and formed two different nations in the territory of present-day Iran. The Medes, who were skilled in astronomy, were the first to gain power in the region. They lived in the northwest and called their realm Media, establishing their capital city at Ecbatana (modern Hamadan).

The Medes did not immediately expel the groups who were already living in the area. Indeed, for some time the Medes paid an annual tax to the Assyrians, whose empire stretched from central Turkey to southern Iraq.

In 612 B.C. a Median leader named Cyaxares took over the Assyrian capital of Nineveh in present-day Iraq. As a result of this conquest, Cyaxares was able to extend his lands almost as far as modern Gorgan, near the eastern coast of the Caspian Sea. In the meantime, the Persians—also an Aryan people from central Asia—settled in southern Iran. The Greek name for the region was Persis, from which Persia is derived.

The Persians established relations with the Elamites, as well as with other domains that bordered their territory. By 625 B.C. the Medes had made the Persian realm a dependent but self-governing territory within Media. In 550 B.C. the balance of power was reversed when the Persians under Cyrus the Great, who had married a Median princess, subdued the Medes and annexed Media to Persia. His dynasty (family of rulers) was called the Achaemenid, after an earlier Persian leader. In time, Cyrus's army conquered lands that stretched from modern Greece to modern Pakistan.

The Persian Empire, starting as a small kingdom in the foothills of southwestern Iran, became a vast world power in the span of a single generation. Cyrus built his capital at Pasargadae, and succeeding kings established a city at Persepolis, near present-day Shiraz. Later Achaemenids developed vast systems of overland travel and expanded opportunities for trade within the region. The empire eventually stretched from the Mediterranean Sea to India and from the Gulf of Oman to the Soviet Union.

After Cyrus's death in about 530 B.C., however, it became evident that, although the empire had grown rapidly, it did not have a stable foundation. Troubles beset the empire because Cyrus's successors could not decide how to choose a new leader. In addition, a series of rebellions, called the Persian Wars, rocked the empire. The worst revolt took place in 500 B.C. when the Ionian Greeks of Asia Minor rebelled.

An animal's head with enlarged nostrils and bulging eyes ornaments the top of a pillar at Persepolis.

Carved beadwork enhances the decoration on a partially preserved artwork at the entrance to Darius's city near present-day Shiraz.

Constructed in the sixth century B.C., Darius's palace and audience hall contain sculptures that depict life at the Persian court.

Lines of soldiers and courtiers march across carved stone slabs that form part of the audience hall at Persepolis. The details of their clothing and weaponry have provided historians with information about ancient Persian customs.

One of the walls of Darius's palace shows a lion—a traditional symbol of strength—attacking a bull.

Defeat of the Persians

The Persian Wars pitted Persia against Greece—two strong powers with conflicting ideologies. Persia was organized as a monarchy in which the king alone was the center of the empire. The democratic communities of Greece had a government that depended on an educated elite within the city-state to make decisions. Darius—who eventually succeeded Cyrus—stopped the Greek revolt in Asia Minor in 494 B.C. But the Greeks defeated other Persian expeditions at Marathon, Salamis, and Plataea.

To destroy the Persian Empire, Philip of Macedon formed a powerful league that joined Macedon—a Greek city-state of the north—with the southern city-states of Sparta and Athens. Philip's son Alexander became his successor, and Alexander's army defeated Persia's troops at Issus in 333 B.C. Two years later, the Persians lost a final battle to Alexander's forces at Granicus.

A silver tetradrachm coin—issued in 323 B.C., the year Alexander the Great died—shows the head of Hercules *(top)* on the front. The back *(bottom)* depicts Zeus (the strongest of the Greek gods) enthroned, holding a royal scepter and an eagle. The Greek lettering translates as "Alexander the king."

A mosaic from the fourth century B.C. illustrates Alexander the Great in battle at Issus. The confrontation between Alexander and Darius III, the last king of the Achaemenid ruling family, signaled the end of the Persian dynasty.

Alexander and the Seleucids

For Persia, the arrival of Alexander signaled the beginning of foreign rule. Alexander's goal was to unite the Greek and Persian civilizations into a single unit. Greek teachers taught 30,000 young men from the best Persian families, and the Macedonian infantry included Persian soldiers. Alexander's dream of unification was interrupted by his early death in 323 B.C. Since he had no heirs, Alexander's empire became divided as his generals competed for control. Seleucus, one of Alexander's generals who had married a Persian woman, took control of the territory of present-day Iran.

The Seleucid dynasty faced problems from lands controlled by Alexander's other generals. The Ptolemyes of Egypt harassed the Seleucids, as did a nomadic people from the newly established eastern realm of Parthia. Forces of the developing Roman Empire also invaded Seleucid holdings. The successors of Seleucus held the region for nearly two centuries, but by the second century B.C. the Parthians under King Mithradates II had absorbed nearly all of the Seleucid kingdom.

The Parthians and the Sasanians

During their 400 years in power, the Parthians adopted much of Greek culture but also encouraged a return to old Persian traditions and customs. They continued the struggle against Rome and kept other invaders out, but they also expanded Persia's boundaries into India and to the frontiers of Egypt.

In A.D. 224 Ardashir, the leader of a small state in what is now Iraq, overthrew the last Parthian king. Ardashir and his descendants, who were called Sasanians, ruled Persian lands from the third to the seventh centuries A.D.

Rome also threatened the security of the Sasanian dynasty. The hereditary priesthood of the Zoroastrian religion (a Persian sect tolerated to varying degrees by previous dynasties) brought needed unity to

Courtesy of James H. Marrinan

The profile *(left)* of the Parthian king Mithradates II (123–88 B.C.) appears on a silver coin minted during his reign. The back of the coin *(right)* shows the king enthroned, with "Mithradates the king" inscribed in Greek letters around the rim.

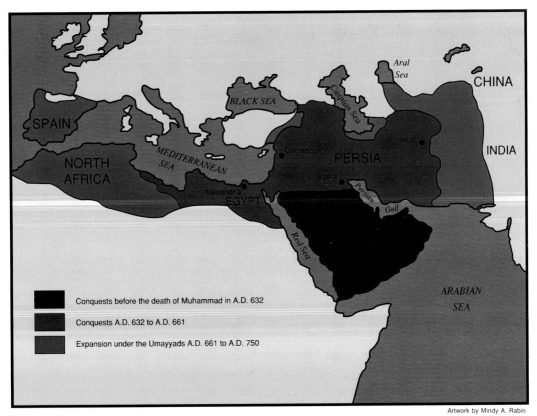

Armies made up of Muslims (members of the Islamic faith) conquered Persia in the mid-seventh century A.D. Their realm eventually stretched from Western Europe to India.

the Sasanians and helped them to withstand threats to their authority. As a result of the support of the Zoroastrians, the Sasanians declared Zoroastrianism to be the national religion.

The Arrival of Arab Armies

Eventually, however, many problems destroyed the Sasanian dynasty. Corruption, a series of weak kings, constant wars with Rome, and an oppressive landholding system that enslaved millions of Persians contributed to the downfall of the kingdom. As a result, Persia became easy prey for an Arabian army that came from present-day Saudi Arabia.

Motivating these fighters was a new faith—Islam—which called for expansion of territory and conversion of non-Islamic peoples. Under their Islamic leader, called a caliph, Arab forces defeated the Sasanians in the mid-seventh century. The Arabs, who carried their Islamic ideas with them, crushed Zoroastrianism and installed Islam as the national religion. Zoroastrianism survived among only a small minority, and Persia became a Muslim country.

In the seventh century, soon after the death of Muhammad—the founder and leader of the Islamic religion—a controversy emerged over how to choose his successors. As a result, two Islamic sects—the Sunnis and the Shiites—developed. Sunnis supported an elected Islamic leadership, while Shiites believed the only true successors to Muhammad were his descendants.

Most Persian groups belonged to the Shiite sect, and their activities constantly threatened the Sunni Umayyad caliphate (territory under Islamic control),

An Indian drawing represents the Mongol conqueror Genghis Khan dividing his empire—which included Persia—among his sons, who are kneeling at his feet.

The Bettmann Archive

which included Persia among its holdings. The Shiites supported a rebellion in A.D. 750 that brought the first Abbasid caliph to power. Abbasid rulers inspired little unity within their far-flung caliphate, and, in time, their hold on Persian lands weakened. As a result, independent kingdoms —such as the Tahirid and Samanid— emerged in the ninth and tenth centuries.

The Seljuk Turks

While local kingdoms came to power and declined, another group—the nomadic Sel-juk Turks from central Asia—began moving into Persia. Persian kings had used the Seljuks as slaves and had trained them to be fearless soldiers and able administrators. In the eleventh century, one group of Seljuks moved south and west into Persia. Although the newcomers subdued local peoples and towns, the Seljuks rarely destroyed these settlements. They usually left administrative matters in the hands of local officials.

During more than a century of Seljuk rule, the arts and sciences thrived. The poet and scientist Omar Khayyam produced his memorable poems and developed a more accurate calendar. Theologians came to the religious schools set up by the Seljuks. After the death of the Seljuk leader Malik-Shah, however, rivalries again divided the kingdom. The weakened realm attracted a new invading force—the Mongols from China.

The Mongol Khans

Sweeping through China in the thirteenth century, the Mongols and their leader Genghis Khan (meaning world conqueror) made their way to the territory of present-day Iran. With a strong and well-trained army, the Mongols conquered the remainder of the Seljuk Empire. Mongol soldiers destroyed cities and towns, killing thousands of people. Indeed, between 1220 and 1258, Persia lost one-quarter of its population to Mongol conquest.

Grandsons and great-grandsons of Genghis Khan ruled parts of Persian territory until the fifteenth century. Although they were harsh military conquerors, the Mongols sometimes were patrons of the arts and opened trade and artistic exchange with Asia. As a result, Persian art took on the delicate techniques of Chinese artisanship.

One of the last Mongol khans, Timur the Lame (called Tamerlane in the West), arrived in Persia from the north. Timur ruled Persia from Samarkand, his capital in Uzbekistan (the modern Uzbek Soviet Socialist Republic). The death of Timur and constant internal rivalry ended the dynasty in the mid-fifteenth century. Thereafter, a Turkoman group called

Born in what is now the Soviet Union, Timur the Lame took over the Mongol leadership in 1370. He and his armies arrived in eastern Persia in about 1385, using the region as a base for other conquests.

Courtesy of Embassy of the Islamic Republic of Iran, Ottawa

A fifteenth-century Persian miniature painting, in a distinctly Chinese style, portrays a mounted warrior slaying a dragon.

Al-Qoyunlu (literally "possessing white sheep"), ruled much of Persia. They established their capital at Tabriz and immediately waged war against the Ottoman Turks, who had control of much of Turkey and the Middle East.

The Safavid Shahs

One of the groups subordinate to Al-Qoyunlu was the Safavids, who lived in eastern Azerbaijan. Early in his reign, Esmail, the leader of the Safavids, began to wage attacks against Al-Qoyunlu. By 1500 Esmail had taken Tabriz and had proclaimed Shiism the state religion.

A powerful neighbor, the Ottoman Empire, advanced east from Asia Minor into Persia. Tabriz fell, and Esmail's successor moved the Safavid capital to the shelter of Qazvin near the Elburz Mountains. From this location, the kingdom began to prosper, despite successors of unpredictable competency.

The fifth of the Safavid shahs, Abbas I, unified the kingdom of Persia in the sixteenth and seventeenth centuries. After moving the capital from Qazvin to Isfahan

Courtesy of Minneapolis Public Library and Information Center

During the reign of the Safavid shahs, many structures — such as Isfahan's Seosepol Bridge with its 33 arches — were built using new technologies and innovative architectural designs.

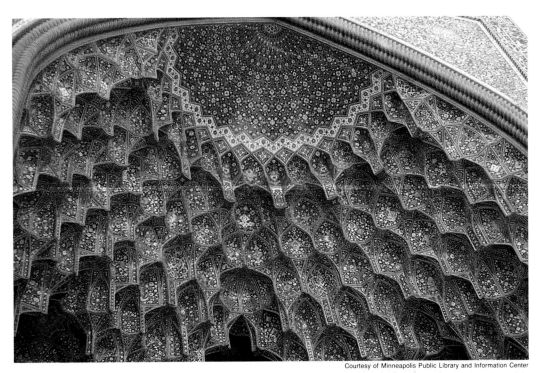

The ceiling of the northern entrance of the seventeenth-century Masjid-i-Shah Mosque in Isfahan displays the intensely geometric nature of the Islamic decorative style.

in 1598, Abbas transformed the site from an underdeveloped city into one of the most beautiful capitals of its day.

The shah made peace with the Ottoman Turks to secure his western and northwestern borders. He reorganized the army and the bureaucracy so that their loyalties were focused on the shah. With his new troops, he quieted his eastern boundary by defeating the Uzbeks of southern Russia. In time, Abbas I was even able to regain many of the lands formerly surrendered to the Ottomans.

In addition to military and political accomplishments, Abbas's reign saw a renewal of the arts. Persian textiles—including carpets, silks, and brocades—became famous for their exquisite colors and designs. Book arts—illustration, calligraphy (ornate handwriting), and bookbinding—flourished under Abbas. Mosques of unique beauty and artistry were built and adorned with fine ceramics and mosaic tiles.

Under Shah Abbas I, book arts—especially calligraphy, or ornate handwriting—thrived.

27

A fresco, or painting on plaster, depicts a court meal in Isfahan at the palace of Shah Abbas I.

The shah also opened his court to Westerners, making a treaty with Britain that gave it the sole right to trade Persian silks. Despite his success as a leader, Abbas chose to maim or kill his sons to prevent them from threatening his rule.

The shahs who succeeded Abbas shared few of his positive qualities and none of his drive. They were more interested in the comforts of their palaces, and their neglect weakened the Safavid realm.

Short-Lived Regimes

In 1722 Afghans surrounded Isfahan, capital of the enfeebled Safavid kingdom. The invaders cut off food supplies and slowly starved the Persians into submission. Shah Sultan Husayn finally gave up his throne and surrendered the city to the Afghan leaders in order to end the siege.

As a result of the shah's abdication, the Safavid dynasty collapsed.

The brief rule of the Afghans ended in 1727, after they were defeated in several battles by a Persian force led by Nader Qoli. Soon after his victories, Nader proclaimed himself shah of Persia. Organizing an expedition, he conquered Afghanistan and then marched eastward to Delhi, India. Among the prizes he captured and brought back to Persia was the jewel-encrusted Peacock Throne.

Nader Shah's rule included huge tax demands and misuse of the land, and after a few years of his reign, a captain of his own guard assassinated him. A successor to Nader, Karim Khan Zand Mohammad, ruled peacefully for 25 years, uniting the nation and healing the wounds of constant conflict. The death of Karim Khan left Persia again in disorder.

The Qajar Dynasty

In 1787 Agha Mohammad Khan, leader of the Qajars, defeated the Persians. The Qajars were a Turkish group that had settled in Armenia during the days of Timur the Lame. They established the capital of their kingdom at Tehran and ruled for nearly 150 years.

The Qajars remained powerful by making alliances and by turning the European powers—particularly Great Britain and Russia—against one another. Western powers needed the new markets and raw materials offered by the untapped Persian lands. Qajar alliances did not last long, and few had a permanent effect on Persia's security. But the Qajars did manage to make their existence a necessity—at least as a focus for negotiations with Western countries.

When the Qajars attacked Afghanistan in 1856, the British tried to oust the Qajar forces from the land that lay between Persia and British-ruled India. Britain's support of Afghanistan and Russia's decision not to send help to Persia forced the Qajar troops to withdraw. The Treaty of Paris in 1857 established Afghanistan's independence and led to later losses of Persian land to Afghanistan.

European Influence

Guided by their own interests, Britain and Russia determined Persia's boundary with Turkey in 1847, with Russia in 1884, and with Baluchistan, which included parts of southwestern Pakistan and eastern Persia, in 1893. To finance itself, the Qajar dynasty gave the British the right to form the Imperial Bank of Persia and to explore for oil. Nearly bankrupt at the end of the nineteenth century, the shah accepted two large loans from Russia that placed Persia's financial future in Russian hands.

The rise of foreign influence caused groups of educated Persians to demand changes. In 1906 merchants, members of the Islamic clergy, and political reformists forced the shah to agree to a constitution that would provide for a national assembly, called the Majlis.

Although one of the primary reasons for the troubles in 1906 was foreign influence, outside interests continued to operate in Persia. An Anglo-Russian agreement in 1907 split much of the region between the British and the Russians, with Russia gaining influence over most of Persia.

A neutral stance in World War I did not prevent Persia from being crisscrossed by Russian, British, and German troops. In the postwar peace conferences, it appeared that Britain would dominate Persia's future. Before the British plan could be enacted, however, Soviet Russia (which had resulted from the 1917 Russian Revolution) and Persia announced a treaty of friendship between the two countries. The treaty cancelled Persia's Russian debts, recognized Persia's access to ports, and

Ahmad Shah (1898–1930) was the last ruler of Iran from the Qajar dynasty.

returned the economic rights it had sold to Russia. In return, Persia promised that it would not become a base of operations for anti-Soviet activities.

A coup d'état in 1921 prevented the treaty from being put into practice. Reza Khan, a general in the Persian Cossack Brigade, led the coup. By 1923 he was prime minister, and the last Qajar shah left the country. In 1926 a special assembly chose Reza Khan—renamed Reza Shah Pahlavi—as the head of a new Persian dynasty.

Reza Shah

Appalled by Persia's underdevelopment, Reza Shah set out to bring Western ways and technology to the nation. His aim was to modernize Iran in order to put it back on the road to greatness. He forced his male subjects to replace their traditional turbans and robes with European suits.

Women no longer wore the veils demanded by Islamic law, a change that caused the clergy to resist the shah's modernization plans. New laws permitted women to go to the movies and to visit cafes for the first time.

To improve transportation, Reza Shah ordered the construction of 1,000 miles of trans-Iranian highways. He also tore down the traditional mud dwellings of Tehran, putting a new, European face on the city. In 1935 the shah changed the official name of the country to Iran (from the word *Aryan,* the name of Iran's early settlers), and he cut Arabic and Turkish words from the Persian language. Iran's glorious past, the shah believed, was an essential element in the nation's plans for the future—a future he wanted to achieve without foreign money or foreign interference.

As a consequence of his long-lived hostility toward Great Britain and the

Artwork by Steven Woods

This version of the official flag of Iran was in use between 1933 and 1958. The green, white, and red stripes respectively stand for prosperity, peace, and the willingness of Iranians to sacrifice their lives for the nation. The lion and the sun are very old Persian symbols, but, during the reign of Mohammad Reza Pahlavi, the lion was drawn in a standing posture with a raised sword in its paw.

Courtesy of Embassy of the Islamic Republic of Iran, Ottawa

Soviet Union, Reza Shah allied himself with Germany at the start of World War II. In 1941 British and Soviet troops occupied Iran and forced the pro-Nazi shah to give up the throne to his son, Mohammad. The Old King, as Reza Shah became known, was deported to South Africa, where he died in 1950.

World War II

During the war, Iran was a vital link in the Allied supply line to the Soviet Union. In 1943 Franklin Roosevelt, Winston Churchill, and Joseph Stalin—the leaders of the Allied countries—met in Tehran. The document they created at the meeting, the Tehran Declaration, pledged respect for the sovereignty and integrity of Iran.

Under the terms of the declaration, foreign troops were to be withdrawn by 1946. Soviet forces stationed in the northern province of East Azerbaijan, however, not only refused to leave but supported pro-Soviet rebels in Azerbaijan and Kurdistan. The Iranian government, backed by the

After deposing Ahmad Shah, Reza Khan became shah of Iran of the Pahlavi dynasty in 1926. His policies vastly changed Iranian society and sowed the seeds of later discontent, particularly among the Islamic clergy.

Independent Picture Service

United Nations and strongly supported by the United States, expelled the Soviet army.

Oil and Nationalism

In the postwar era, the oil rights that Iran had sold to foreign companies grew in importance. The British had been drilling for oil in Persia since the early twentieth century and had struck a rich field in 1908—the first discovery of oil in the Middle East. The Anglo-Persian Oil Company was founded in 1909 and fit in well with Britain's decision to change from coal-fueled to oil-powered naval vessels.

At the end of World War II, U.S. and British oil companies asked for further oil drilling rights in southeastern Iran, and the Soviet Union requested rights in the north. The Majlis rejected these requests

Courtesy of USASC

The heads of the main Allied countries in World War II—the Soviet Union's Joseph Stalin *(left)*, U.S. president Franklin D. Roosevelt *(center)*, and British prime minister Winston Churchill *(right)*—met at the end of 1943 in Tehran. Among other decisions contained in the Tehran Declaration was an affirmation of Iran's sovereignty.

Iranian prime minister Mohammad Mosaddeq closed the British-built refinery at Abadan in 1951 after nationalizing (changing from private to government ownership) Iran's oil industry.

in an effort to limit the amount of foreign influence on Iran's affairs.

The period that followed witnessed the growth of Iranian nationalism and the rise to power of Mohammad Mosaddeq— leader of the National Front party. The young shah, Mohammad Reza Pahlavi, had appointed Mosaddeq prime minister in 1951.

Supported by the Majlis, Mosaddeq nationalized (changed to government ownership) the British-run oil industry in Iran. The prime minister also sponsored a law that removed the oil industry from British control. Most British citizens left Iran, and the huge Abadan refinery was closed. For two years, the Mosaddeq government refused to change its position on nationalization of the oil industry. As a result, production of oil fell drastically, and widespread unemployment and unrest occurred.

Mosaddeq had wide experience in Iranian politics, serving as provincial governor and as head of several royal ministries under Ahmad Shah. From 1927 to 1944— years during which Mosaddeq did not hold public office—he vocally opposed the policies of Reza Shah Pahlavi. Between 1944 and 1953 Mosaddeq occupied a seat in the legislature. After his downfall in 1953, the former prime minister remained either in prison or confined to his house until his death in 1967.

33

The Fall of Mosaddeq and Its Aftermath

Because of the internal unrest, Mosaddeq asked the shah for unlimited control of the government. At first the shah refused and named a new prime minister. Faced with public rioting at the removal of Mosaddeq, however, the shah reappointed him, giving Mosaddeq the requested powers. In 1952 the prime minister authorized laws to strictly censor news, to prohibit labor strikes, and to suspend elections to the Majlis. Economic difficulties increased, partly because Western oil companies refused to buy Iranian oil.

Support for Mosaddeq waned in the Majlis, which he had tried to abolish, and in 1953 the shah dismissed him. Mosaddeq refused to relinquish his office and announced that he had overthrown the shah. The shah left Iran, and for four days riots and unrest spread throughout Tehran.

The army—under General Fazlollah Zahedi, who was the shah's next choice for prime minister—supported the shah and arrested Mosaddeq and his followers. British and U.S. agencies both secretly and openly assisted the army, ensuring the success of the shah's forces against Mosaddeq. The shah returned to Tehran, and Zahedi became prime minister.

No longer having to compete with Mosaddeq for power, Mohammad Reza Pahlavi began to centralize his authority and to diminish the power of the Majlis. One of the new government's first acts was to mend its relations with Western countries.

In 1954, with U.S. help, Iran and eight oil companies signed a 25-year contract to operate the former Anglo-Iranian plant on Abadan Island. The document arranged for the British company to be paid $70 million as compensation for its loss of the oil industry facility and for Iran to be allotted 50 percent of all earnings from the new business. This arrangement made it possible to revitalize the oil industry, and the increased revenues funded a vast development project within Iran.

Mohammad Reza Pahlavi

In the late 1950s the shah instituted the first of several methods to maintain his authority. In 1957 he created a national security and intelligence organization called SAVAK, which monitored political activity and the press. Arrests and torture of prisoners by SAVAK agents were frequent and caused a high degree of antigovernment feeling among various elements of Iranian society. An elite group of military and civilian employees remained faithful to the shah, who rewarded their loyalty with large salaries.

In 1962 the shah declared a land reform and redistribution plan—called the White Revolution. Land was taken out of the hands of large landowners, who then could no longer fine their tenants by collecting

Independent Picture Service

In 1954 the shah's representative Ali Amini signed an agreement with eight foreign oil companies that gave Iran 50 percent of the profits generated by its oil resources.

Mohammad Reza Pahlavi – seen here opening the Iranian national assembly in the 1970s – diminished the power of the legislature throughout his reign.

most of the harvests as rent. In addition, electoral reform was enacted, and Iranian women voted for the first time in 1963. Later the government made efforts to increase the literacy rate and to improve health standards.

But sudden attempts to modernize and Westernize Iran drew criticism from traditional landowners and from Shiite leaders. In 1963 the shah's forces attacked the headquarters of the clergy near Qom and took the ayatollah Ruhollah Khomeini from his home, moving him to Tehran. This move was meant to remove the focus of antigovernment sentiment. The next day demonstrations against Khomeini's imprisonment erupted in Tehran and other cities. A year later Khomeini was freed, and he left the country, moving first to Iraq and then to France.

The 1960s and 1970s were decades of economic growth and wider international involvement for Iran. Long supported by the West, especially the United States, Iran sought to establish more widespread friendships with countries not allied with the United States. The shah visited the Soviet Union and developed closer links—including the founding of the Organization of Petroleum Exporting Countries (OPEC) in 1960—with many other Arab nations.

Events of the 1970s

To centralize his authority further, the shah decreed a one-party system in 1975. All other political parties were banned. The shah's response to internal dissatisfaction became increasingly repressive, and human rights organizations reported numerous violations, carried out mostly by members of SAVAK.

The vast oil profits coming to Iran paid for internal development projects and strengthened Iran's position abroad. The population continued to increase, and thousands moved from rural to urban areas, especially to the capital. Among traditional Shiite Islamic groups, a feeling prevailed that plans for development and modernization were growing too rapidly. Demonstrations erupted against the government in 1978, and by late autumn Iran was nearly in a state of civil war.

In late 1978 the shah declared military rule, and his forces attacked protesters in downtown Tehran. Martial law proved ineffective, however. Unable to rule, the shah departed for Egypt, leaving the government in the hands of his prime minister. On February 1, 1979, Ruhollah Khomeini returned to Iran from exile and appointed Mehdi Bazargan, a moderate civilian, as the prime minister of an Islamic revolutionary government.

The Islamic Republic

A national public vote held in April 1979 enabled Khomeini to establish a Shiite Islamic republic and eventually to enact a new constitution. The regime executed many members of SAVAK and other supporters of the shah. Organized according to Islamic ideals, the government repealed the modern divorce laws and again required women to wear the chador, or veil, in accordance with Islamic law. The new leaders suppressed Western influences, and many Western-educated Iranians fled the country.

In November 1979 supporters of the revolution took over the U.S. embassy in Tehran and captured 66 hostages, 52 of whom were held until January 20, 1981. The act was said to be a response to continued U.S. support for the shah, who died in Egypt in 1980. After the Islamic repub-

Courtesy of Embassy of the Islamic Republic of Iran, Ottawa

Fire engulfs a picture of the shah during the 1979 Islamic revolution in Iran.

Courtesy of Embassy of the Islamic Republic of Iran, Ottawa

Graffiti in both the English and Persian languages expressed hostility toward the presence of U.S. officials and businesspeople in Iran. This sentiment eventually led to the seizure of the U.S. embassy in Tehran in 1979.

Courtesy of Embassy of the Islamic Republic of Iran, Ottawa

The shah declared martial law (rule by the military) in 1978. The move brought the shah's soldiers and members of the Iranian public into frequent conflict.

Courtesy of Embassy of the Islamic Republic of Iran, Ottawa

A poster on a Tehran building celebrates the return to Iran of Ayatollah Ruhollah Khomeini in 1979.

Courtesy of Embassy of the Islamic Republic of Iran, Ottawa

A soldier of the revolutionary guards displays his loyalty to the ayatollah.

lic's first elections in January 1980, the clergy dominated the Iranian legislature. Without legislative support, the republic's first president, Abol Hasan Bani-Sadr—who opposed the holding of the U.S. embassy—was unable to govern and lost Khomeini's confidence. As a result, he went into exile in France and founded an opposition movement to overthrow the Iranian government.

Violent confrontations erupted between supporters of the government's Islamic Revolutionary party (IRP) and the mujahedeen, who wanted a nonreligious republic. Bombings in 1982 killed several IRP leaders, including the president who succeeded Bani-Sadr.

Conflict with Iraq

A 1975 pact between Iran and Iraq settled disagreements regarding access to the Shatt al-Arab and ownership of several islands in the Persian Gulf. In 1980, however, the Iraqi government demanded a revision of the agreement and independence for a Sunni Muslim minority in Khuzestan. The Iranian government rejected these demands, and in September 1980 Iraqi forces invaded Khuzestan, occupying much of the province.

By the end of the year, Iranian troop advances had produced a stalemate with the Iraqi forces. The conflict continued, causing regional and international concern over the threat to oil resources and to governments of the Persian Gulf area.

In the mid-1980s the war still received public support in Iran, in part because Iranians regarded the conflict as one between the Shiite and Sunni branches of Islam. In addition, Iranian troops had successfully captured Iraqi territory near the Shatt al-Arab, hampering Iraq's ability to finance its military activities. Arab states in the region watched the war from the sidelines and feared that Iran would export its radical Shiite Islamic government to their own countries.

Beginning in 1987, Iran experienced some setbacks. Frequent bombings of oil tankers and other ships occurred in the gulf. Western armed forces—notably those of the United States—cooperated with noncombatant Arab states to protect vessels trying to pass through the gulf. On several occasions, U.S. and Iranian forces clashed in the region, resulting in loss of life and property damage.

The Arab League (an organization of Arab nations dedicated to strengthening Arab unity) called for Iran and Iraq to accept a UN-sponsored cease-fire agreement. Iraq, which was militarily weak at that point, consented to the resolution; Iran did not. As a result, support for Iran within the Arab world weakened.

In 1988 Iran launched a new offensive against Basra, the Iraqi port at the mouth of the Shatt al-Arab. The attack failed to take the city, and many Iranians died in battle. In addition, Iraq began to use internationally outlawed chemical weapons (poison gas) to fight Iran—a move that intimidated Iran's relatively young and inexperienced soldiers.

By mid-1988 Iran lacked sufficient weaponry and troop enlistments to continue the war. Taking the advice of his top officials—including legislative spokesperson Ali Akbar Hashemi Rafsanjani—Khomeini accepted the UN resolution for a cease-fire. The measure included arrangements both for troop withdrawals and for the exchange of prisoners of war.

Recent Events

Iran's financial situation seemed to stabilize in the early 1980s. But increased imports of foodstuffs and weapons have created a drain on an economy that is already stricken by declining world demand for oil.

Large-scale executions—often as punishment for antigovernment activities—widespread censorship, support for terrorist activities in Lebanon and elsewhere, and arbitrary arrests have damaged Iran's global reputation. Political opposition at times has been allowed and at other times has been curtailed, depending on political currents in Khomeini's support groups.

UPI/Reuters Photo

Captured Iraqi soldiers wait in a prisoner-of-war camp in Ahvaz, southwestern Iran. Including civilians, over 500,000 Iranians and Iraqis died in the conflict, which began in 1980. The UN cease-fire resolution—accepted by Iraq in 1987 and by Iran in 1988—provides for the exchange of captured soldiers.

In response to Iran's missile attacks on Kuwaiti ships, U.S. Navy vessels shelled an Iranian oil drilling platform in the Persian Gulf in October 1987.

Rivalry among factions weakens the unity of the government, and internal divisions are the greatest threat to the stability of the regime.

One of the most active factions includes Rafsanjani and the prime minister, Hosein Musavi-Khamenei. They lead a group within the Iranian government that wants to reestablish relations with other nations in order to solve some of the country's economic problems. (This view resulted in a secret arms agreement with the United States in 1986.)

Rafsanjani and Musavi-Khamenei also argue for less control of the government by the clergy—a position that pits them against Hussein Ali Montazeri, Khomeini's designated successor. Despite the hopeful sign of impending peace, Iran needs a long period of recovery to address its serious economic and political problems.

Government

As an Islamic republic, Iran supports three main ideas: rule by Allah (the Arabic word for God); strict observance of the sacred writings of the Koran; and support for the leadership of the Shiite clergy. At the head of the clergy is a faqih—a scholar who is well versed in Islamic ideas and Koranic law. The constitution identifies Ruhollah Khomeini as the first faqih of the Islamic Republic of Iran, giving him powers and rights that outweigh those of any appointed or elected government official. The faqih appoints Islamic religious thinkers and judicial authorities and chooses his own successor.

Although elected by direct vote to a four-year term, the president does not rule the country independently of the Islamic leadership. The prime minister, who is nominated by the president, and the ministers, who are nominated by the prime minister, also answer to the clergy, many of whom hold positions in the various government branches.

Legislative power rests with the Majlis, whose members are directly elected by the Iranian people. The 270 representatives serve four-year terms and may increase in number as the population grows. A council that guards the constitution makes

39

Courtesy of Embassy of the Islamic Republic of Iran, Ottawa

Ruhollah Khomeini is descended from the prophet Muhammad and has come to be called an imam (an intermediary between Allah and Shiite Muslims). As a result of his position, Khomeini's decisions have both religious and political force for Shiites.

certain that the Majlis enacts laws that do not contradict the Koran. When the members of the council decide that a law is contrary to the Koran, they return it to the Majlis for reconsideration. The council is made up of six clergy and six lawyers, who are each elected to six-year terms.

The Constitution of 1979 provides for a judicial council to carry out the laws of the land, especially the sharia, or Islamic laws. Its members are elected to five-year terms of office. A tribunal under the supervision of the judicial council investigates complaints of the public against the government. The judicial council strictly enforces the sharia, including the often-used death penalty.

For administrative purposes, the country is divided into 24 provinces called *ostans.* These units are subdivided into 172 counties, each of which is under the authority of a governor, who is appointed by the central government.

Artwork by Steven Woods

After the revolution of 1979, Iran changed the design—but not the colors—of its flag. In the center of the white stripe are two contours of a red globe, within which are depicted an upright sword and four crescents—the symbols of strength and Islamic faith, respectively. Along the bottom of the green stripe and the top of the red stripe are the words "God is Great" in Farsi, the national language. The inscription is repeated 22 times—a reference to the twenty-second day in the Islamic month of Bahman (February 11, 1979) when the revolution succeeded in replacing the shah with an Islamic government.

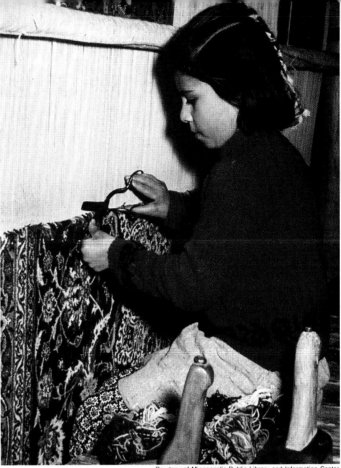

A young Iranian weaves a Persian rug by hand, using techniques that have not changed in centuries.

3) The People

Every conquering group that has come to Iran has changed the ethnic makeup of the population. As a result, today's Iranians represent many ancestries. For example, Iran includes sizable Turkish and Arab minorities, as well as groups like the Kurds, the Lur, and the Baluchi, who speak Indo-European languages.

With 51.9 million people, Iran has a population density of about 75 persons per square mile, which is sparse compared to Turkey's ratio of 169 and Great Britain's of 605. About half of the people live in nearly 50,000 small villages scattered throughout the country. Roughly three million Iranians are nomads, including the Kurds, the Lur, and the Bakhtiaris.

Ethnic Groups

Although the term Persian has been widely used to refer to all of Iran's population, the name best describes a group of people who speak Indo-Iranian dialects and who live in the central plateau. Even with these limitations, however, Persians still represent the largest ethnic group in Iran. Most Persians either live in cities or cluster in developed areas where farming provides a settled living.

One-third of the Middle East's entire population of Kurds live in Iran, where they form 8 percent of the total number of Iranians. The Kurds reside mainly in the Zagros Mountains of northwestern Iran. Language and ethnic customs relate the Kurds to the Persians, although scientists consider them to be descendants of the original Medes. The Iranian Kurds have revolted against the established order on several occasions. After the 1979 Shiite revolution, the Sunni Kurds demanded independence, and only recently have relations between the government and the Kurdish religious minority grown calm.

The Lur, numbering about one million, live in the west near the Iraqi border. The closest of any present-day Iranians to the original central Asian settlers, the Lur are divided between year-round residents of villages and migratory herders. Also nomadic and related to the Lur are the Bakhtiaris, who live in an area stretching from Lorestan to Khuzestan near the Iraqi border.

The Baluchi are linked to peoples that inhabit Pakistan and Afghanistan. In Iran they live in the Makran region of the southeast and form a minority religious population because they are Sunni, not Shiite, Muslims.

Social Customs

In Iran the honor and unity of the family are more important than all other social bonds. A father or husband is head of the

Independent Picture Service

Kurdish villagers meet on the main road that runs through their settlement, which lies near Maku in northwestern Iran.

In northeastern Iran, domed roofs provide protection from the extreme heat of the sun.

clan and has great influence and power in all decisions that affect the family. One's place in the family—determined by age and sex—underlies Iran's social structure. Males have more formal authority than females, and an older person dominates a younger one.

Since inheritance is passed through men, they are the principal property holders and generally choose marriage partners for the unmarried women of their families. Often people who are related to one another will live in their own section of a village, and cousins may marry each other under Islamic law.

Villages are the most important territorial units for most Iranians, but village inhabitants often divide into rival groups and social classes. Among nomadic peoples, territorial claims rest on rights to winter and summer grazing for their herds. During frequent negotiations with neighbors and the government, nomadic groups may shift their allegiances from leader to leader

Two young shepherds watch their flock. Livestock raising is the main occupation of many rural Iranian families.

43

THE STATUS OF WOMEN

Under the Pahlavi shahs, women's rights had been recognized to some degree. Tehran University admitted women soon after its founding in the mid-1930s. In 1936 the government banned the veil, a traditional symbol of Muslim modesty for women. Women gained the right to vote in 1963, after which they could also occupy public offices.

Under Islamic law, which guides the clergy-run government of Iran, women hold a less visible position in society than they did before the revolution. Women are encouraged to cover themselves with the chador, a head-to-foot garment including a veil that hides them from public view.

Courtesy of UNICEF

Iranian women have resisted efforts in the last decade to undo the gains they achieved under the twentieth-century shahs. Although in much smaller numbers, women still participate in the public work force.

Courtesy of UNICEF

In the Islamic republic, Iranian women have largely stepped out of the public eye. The government encourages them to return to traditional domestic lifestyles, which include collecting the family's water supply from local streams.

They are not allowed to participate in sports or to attend science classes, and they cannot use public transportation or other public facilities that may bring them into contact with men.

Changes in Iran's educational system —which the clergy believed was too non-religious and too Westernized—have prevented many women from going to school. The Islamic government has banned most female teachers from pursuing their jobs and has encouraged women to resume their traditional roles in Islamic society. Nevertheless, the Khomeini regime has not denied women the right to vote.

Religion

The spread of the Muslim religion after its founding by Muhammad was rapid in the seventh and eighth centuries, and it soon

44

in the hope of securing greater advantage in the grazing arrangements.

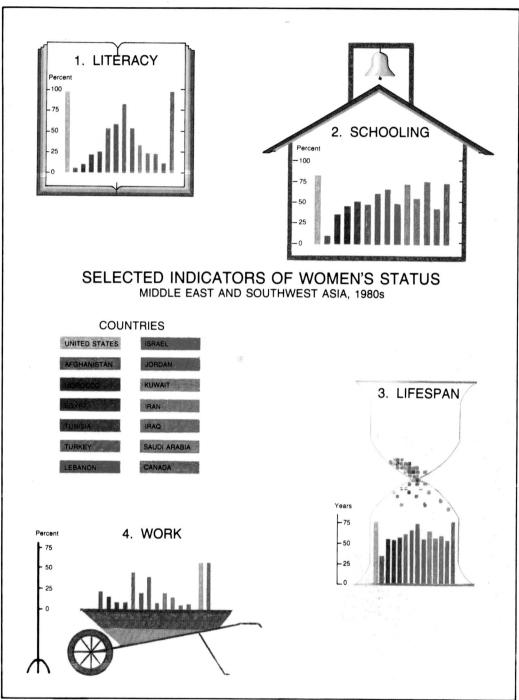

SELECTED INDICATORS OF WOMEN'S STATUS
MIDDLE EAST AND SOUTHWEST ASIA, 1980s

1. LITERACY

2. SCHOOLING

3. LIFESPAN

4. WORK

COUNTRIES

UNITED STATES	ISRAEL
AFGHANISTAN	JORDAN
MOROCCO	KUWAIT
EGYPT	IRAN
TUNISIA	IRAQ
TURKEY	SAUDI ARABIA
LEBANON	CANADA

Artwork by Carol F. Barrett

Depicted in this chart are factors relating to the status of women in the Middle East and southwest Asia. Graph 1, labeled Literacy, shows the percentage of adult women who can read and write. Graph 2 illustrates the proportion of school-aged girls who actually attend elementary and secondary schools. Graph 3 depicts the life expectancy of female babies at birth. Graph 4 shows the percentage of women in the income-producing work force. Data taken from *Women in the World: An International Atlas,* 1986 and from *Women . . . A World Survey,* 1985.

Five times each day, faithful Muslims
kneel in prayer, facing toward the
holy city of Mecca in Saudi Arabia.

Courtesy of United Nations

dominated lands stretching from Spain to
India. A split over the question of succession to the Islamic leadership created two
main branches, or sects, of Islam—the
Shiites and the Sunnis. More than 98 percent of Iranians belong to the Shiite sect
of the Islamic religion.

A major feature of Shiism revolves
around the succession to the Islamic
leadership. An imam, such as Ruhollah
Khomeini, follows in the footsteps of
Muhammad and must deeply understand
and strictly obey the Koran. This ability
will mark him as both the spiritual and

worldly leader of the Shiite community.
For Sunni Muslims, an imam is one who
leads other Muslims in prayer. This dif-
ference in the imam's role and authority
harks back to the original split in the
seventh century.

Shiite Muslims must support five Islamic principles and seven pillars of Islam.
The seven Shiite pillars include fasting
during the holy month of Ramadan, dona-
tions to the poor, daily prayer, and belief
in jihad (holy war).

In general, the Islamic government in
Iran does not tolerate minority faiths, but

An inscription in Farsi commemorates the resting place of Imam Reza, the eighth of twelve holy imams revered by Muslims. For Shiites, imams provide both worldly and religious guidance.

some—including Judaism and Christianity —continue to exist. One of the most colorful religions in Iran is Bahaism, a relatively new faith that originated in Persia in the nineteenth century. The Khomeini regime has forbidden the Bahai to practice their religion.

Language and Literature

Persian (also called Farsi), the principal language of Iran, is of Indo-European origin—that is, it is related to most languages of Europe and southern Asia. Among the other Middle Eastern languages spoken in the country are Kurdish, various forms of Turkish, and Arabic.

Persian is very old, dating back to the seventh century B.C. Some written documents survive, the most important of which are from the Sasanian period.

Imam Reza, who died in A.D. 819, is one of Islam's most important religious figures. His tomb in Mashhad, Iran, is a place of pilgrimage for many Muslims.

A nineteenth-century painting depicts the Persian poet Sadi, who was born in Shiraz in about 1213 but who spent much of his life in Iraq and Jerusalem. His works were among the first examples of Persian literature introduced to Europe.

Farsi, also called Persian, is an Indo-European language, not an Arabic one. This illuminated panel of Farsi calligraphy is by an eighteenth-century artisan.

A mausoleum (above-ground tomb) in Shiraz commemorates Hafez, the fourteenth-century poet who wrote the *Divan,* a collection of about 700 poems that are noted for the beauty of their verse. In Persian Hafez means "one who knows the Koran by heart."

Persian is second only to Arabic as the language of Islam, and for a long time it was the means of spreading culture and literature to a large region from China to Turkey. Today Persian is spoken in Iran, Afghanistan, and parts of Turkey.

The city of Shiraz is associated with the greatest Persian literature. It was home of two of the country's best-loved poets—Sadi and Hafez—who lived in the thirteenth and fourteenth centuries, respectively. Sadi's masterpiece, *Golestan* (The Rose Garden), combines prose and poetry. Hafez wrote the *Divan,* which, along with the Koran and the collection of ideas laid down by Islamic prophets and the ayatollah Khomeini, is most often found in Iranian households. Of all the Persian poets, however, Westerners are probably most familiar with Omar Khayyam, an eleventh-century mathematician, astronomer, and author, who is best known as the author of the *Rubaiyat.*

An Iranian silversmith *(above)* **exhibits the technique that produces exquisitely engraved artworks, such as this heavily ornamented tray** *(top).*

The Arts

Calligraphy is one of the main art forms in Iran. Artists who copy the Koran in ornate fashion are highly regarded, and they

have created a number of calligraphic styles. One of the best-known forms of Iranian art is the miniature, a painting of great detail on a very small scale. This art form was exported to other cultures and sometimes was used to keep historical records of early civilizations.

The origin of Persian rug making dates back to early times, when nomadic Seljuks brought their rug techniques to Persia. Using special knots dating from the Middle Ages, Iranian craftspeople produce carpets of unusual design and quality. The worldwide fame of Persian rugs is due to the delicacy of their knotting, the novelty of their designs, and the durability of their colors. Different regions develop patterns that use distinctive motifs and special dyes. Most carpets are made of either silk or wool.

Since the Koran forbids Muslims to create any human images, the magnificent mosques of Iran are decorated with geometric designs. These forms of art include

An Iranian sits on a rocky hill where he has arranged recently washed Persian rugs to dry. Most rugs made in Iran are rectangular with a border around the four sides and a center space, called a field, where a single image or a repeated pattern completes the composition.

Courtesy of Minneapolis Public Library and Information Center *khatam*—strips of wood, ivory, and bone joined together to make geometrical shapes —as well as enameling, metalwork, leatherwork, and ceramics. Khatam was originally used to decorate furniture, doors, and wooden panels in mosques and palaces. Today it is limited to picture frames, boxes, and jewelry. Enameling, the art of decorating a metal surface with bright colors, is widely used in Iran, mainly in Isfahan. Craftspeople draw from Arabic designs and produce bowls, plates, and boxes with delicate patterns.

Metalwork—in the form of plates, vases, and trays—has survived in Shiraz and Isfahan, where artists use copper and other metals for cutting and engraving. Leatherwork is highly regarded and is used to decorate book bindings and handbags.

Courtesy of Carl Purcell/Agency for International Development

A young girl carries her homework to school. Only about 40 percent of Iranian women can read and write, while 62 percent of the nation's men are literate.

Education

Roughly 47.5 percent of Iranians are literate, but more men than women can read and write. Most Iranians receive a primary-school education, and over 20 percent have had some secondary-school training.

Most primary and secondary schools are state-operated, but students may receive grants to attend private schools. Elementary and university education is free, and small fees are charged for state-run secondary schools. Textbooks are issued free to children in the primary grades. The Free Islamic University and the International University of Islamic Studies were organized following the 1979 revolution.

Religious education is now taking precedence over nonreligious education, and

Courtesy of Embassy of the Islamic Republic of Iran, Ottawa

This oil-painted book cover imitates the shape and style of Persian rugs.

51

funding for secular (nonreligious) programs is greatly reduced. The enrollment at Islamic schools of higher education in Qom, the center of Islamic studies, is growing at a fast pace.

Health

Iranians maintain a high birth rate, with over 45 new infants being born every year for each 1,000 people in the population. At the 1988 growth rate of 3.2 percent, Iran's population could double in 21 years. By the year 2000 the country's total population could reach more than 70 million. Iran's growing population makes it difficult for the government to provide adequate food supplies and health care.

Infant mortality rates—113 deaths per 1,000 live births—are average for southern Asia but are worse than Western figures. The eradication of smallpox and bubonic plague and the near elimination of malaria and cholera have helped extend life expectancy, which was 57 years in 1988. Shortages of medical personnel and supplies, especially in rural areas, are a continuing problem.

About half of Iran's citizens are urban dwellers, and recent immigrations to the cities have caused housing shortages. Central heating is not common, despite winter temperatures that in Tehran average below freezing. Kerosene, wood, coal, and charcoal are often burned for heat, causing severe air pollution and an unhealthy environment in and around the large cities.

Food and Clothing

The staple food of Iranians is rice, especially the long-grained variety, and the national drink is tea. Rice spiced with Indian mango (a tropical fruit) is often served with an egg broken over it or with herbs, such as saffron, and bits of mutton. Iranians usually eat bread with all of their meals.

A typical dinner may consist of a thick soup, rice, vegetables, and yogurt. A popular local dish consists of chunks of mutton covered with a syrupy sauce made

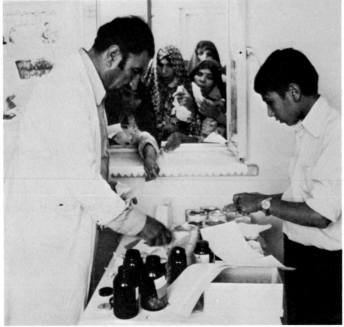

Patients wait in line to receive their prescriptions at an Iranian pharmacy.

Courtesy of UNICEF

This Iranian girl prepares her morning tea, which is taken in a glass with a large lump of sugar as a sweetener. Although women are encouraged to cover themselves, this rule does not apply to girls until they reach puberty.

with pomegranate juice. Vegetable leaves stuffed with rice, as well as skewered meat or fish cooked over a grill, are also favorites in Iran. Iranians are fond of sweet flavors—such as honey and glazed fruits—and they sometimes sip tea through a sugar cube clenched in the jaw.

People who live in urban areas continue to wear Western-style clothing, although women have adopted the chador as a full-length covering. Some men dress in the long flowing robes and turbans that form part of traditional Islamic dress.

In rural regions, men may wear roughly woven shirts and baggy trousers. Sometimes an outer garment is also worn. Village women often dress in clothing that fits their daily tasks, which usually revolve around farming or herding. They wear loose blouses and trousers and cover their heads with scarves.

Wearing a traditional Muslim veil, a woman from the Sabzevar region of northeastern Iran carries water home from the local well.

Workers gather at a washing pool, where they relax and bathe. Iran's economy includes public, cooperative, and private sectors; most Iranians participate at the cooperative or private level as farm laborers, farmers, or merchants.

4) The Economy

Until the late 1970s, Iran's economy was growing, and the incomes of some Iranians nearly doubled between the late 1960s and the late 1970s. The 1979 revolution—followed by the outbreak of the Iran-Iraq war and declining world demand for oil—greatly reduced the nation's earlier rate of economic growth. Nevertheless, Khomeini's government has continued to depend on oil for its national income, getting 48 percent of its revenues from petroleum sales. In the 1980s agriculture and mining each contributed about 18 percent of the gross domestic product (the total value of

goods and services produced by a country in a year). About 21 percent came from taxes, and 7 percent resulted from investments.

Iran's economy revolves around three sectors—public, cooperative, and private. The public sector consists of all large industries involving trade, banking, mining, insurance, energy and irrigation projects, transportation, and communications. The cooperative sector includes production and distribution of food, and the private group is made up of small-scale farmers and urban merchants.

Oil and Mining

Iran is potentially the largest producer of oil in the Middle East. Despite the problems associated with declining oil prices, Iran remains among the top five producers in the world. Output dropped after the 1979 revolution, however, from over six million barrels a day in 1975 to only about two million a day in the mid-1980s.

Iran's known oil reserves are believed to constitute about one-tenth of the world's supply. Exploration and production are concentrated in the southwest, although petroleum has also been discovered in Qom, in the central desert areas, and under the waters of the Persian Gulf.

Natural gas, another valuable asset, is found in the Elburz Mountains and in Khorasan province. Reserves are estimated at 20 percent of the world's total.

Independent Picture Service

A foreign-owned oil tanker waits to leave one of Iran's ports. Despite war damage and declining oil profits, Iran continues to get most of its national income from oil exports.

Independent Picture Service

An offshore Iranian drilling barge lies in the Persian Gulf, a strategic region for the nation's petroleum industry.

Independent Picture Service

Iranian technicians ease the movement of an oil drill.

55

As a conveyor belt brings them containers of newly refined oil, two workers stack the cans in neat rows at a factory in Kermanshah.

Pipelines serve the cities of Tehran, Kashan, Isfahan, Shiraz, Mashhad, and Ahvaz.

A wide variety of mineral deposits exist in addition to oil. Coal is mined in fairly large quantities near Tehran, and iron ore is extracted near Arak and in southern Kerman province. Other metals and metal ores of some importance are manganese, zinc, copper, lead, and chromium. Iran mines valuable deposits of rock salt, sulfates, and other raw materials for chemical production.

Quarries that produce stone for building and gypsum (used in making plaster) exist on a large scale; alabaster and marble are found in lesser quantities. Gemstones include emeralds and topazes, and carnelians and turquoises are important semiprecious stones.

Industry

Less than 20 years ago, big or complex products were not manufactured in Iran. Even in the factories, workers did everything by hand using simple tools. After the shah's reform program began in 1963, however, the country's new production projects encouraged foreign firms to invest large amounts of money in Iran. Isfahan built the largest textile mill in Iran, as well as a large sugar mill, a cement factory, and a huge steel mill. In Tehran, where workers once built buses by hand, a new plant began to mass-produce Iran's cars, with more than 60 percent of the necessary parts produced locally.

After the 1979 revolution, the framework of the industrial sector still existed and was able to produce goods. Iran's principal manufactured products include cement, foodstuffs, textiles, carpets, vegetable oil, and soap. Factories also turn out furniture, machine tools, firearms, sugar, tea, soft drinks, caviar, leather footwear, and petroleum products.

Mass production methods, however, have not been applied to the making of carpets and rugs. To preserve this national heritage, artisans still weave these products by hand on simple looms. The most popular carpets come from the cities of Tabriz, Kerman, Arak, Kashan, Isfahan, Shiraz, and Hamadan. Isfahan is the historic textile manufacturing center, but in recent years Tehran has also begun to turn out cotton fabrics.

HEROIN AND OPIUM PRODUCTION

In the mid-1980s between 400 and 600 tons of opium poppies were grown in Iran per year. The poppies in their rough form are used as opium; after refinement, the poppies become heroin. Both drugs may be smoked, eaten, or injected into the bloodstream and are highly addictive. Use of the drugs can lead to malnutrition, breathing problems, and low blood pressure.

The Islamic government in Iran has discouraged the production of narcotics by imposing stiff punishments—including the death penalty—for those convicted of drug trafficking. Laboratories that refine the poppies are located near Tabriz and Tehran, as well as along Iran's Turkish border. Most Iranian drugs are smuggled through Turkey and then go to Eastern Europe for sale in Western Europe and North America. In addition, producers find users within Iran to support the drug industry.

At a textile factory in Isfahan, an Iranian laborer prepares the automatic thread-winding machines.

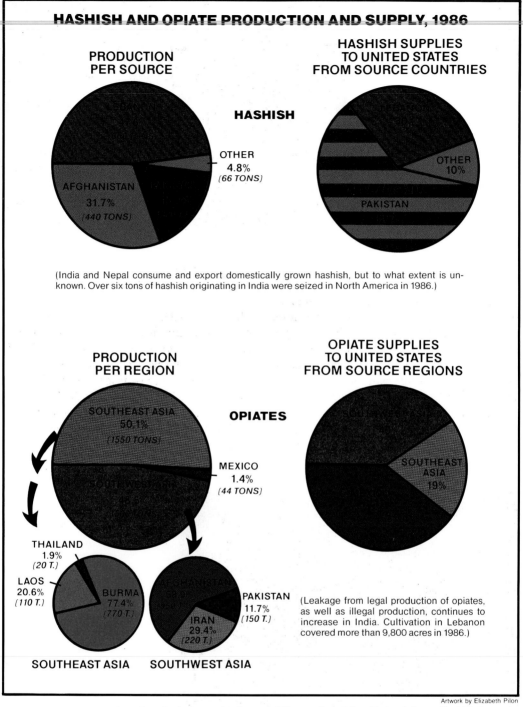

HASHISH AND OPIATE PRODUCTION AND SUPPLY, 1986

PRODUCTION PER SOURCE

HASHISH SUPPLIES TO UNITED STATES FROM SOURCE COUNTRIES

HASHISH

LEBANON

OTHER
4.8%
(66 TONS)

AFGHANISTAN
31.7%
(440 TONS)

OTHER
10%

PAKISTAN

(India and Nepal consume and export domestically grown hashish, but to what extent is unknown. Over six tons of hashish originating in India were seized in North America in 1986.)

PRODUCTION PER REGION

OPIATE SUPPLIES TO UNITED STATES FROM SOURCE REGIONS

OPIATES

SOUTHEAST ASIA
50.1%
(1550 TONS)

MEXICO
1.4%
(44 TONS)

SOUTHEAST
ASIA
19%

THAILAND
1.9%
(20 T.)

LAOS
20.6%
(110 T.)

BURMA
77.4%
(770 T.)

AFGHANISTAN

PAKISTAN
11.7%
(150 T.)

IRAN
29.4%
(220 T.)

(Leakage from legal production of opiates, as well as illegal production, continues to increase in India. Cultivation in Lebanon covered more than 9,800 acres in 1986.)

SOUTHEAST ASIA   SOUTHWEST ASIA

Artwork by Elizabeth Pilon

These pie charts depict data about both the production and U.S. supplies of two kinds of drugs. Hashish is a substance taken from the *Cannabis sativa* plant, which also is a source of marijuana. Opiates are drugs that come from opium poppies *(Papaver somniferum)*, mostly in the refined forms of opium and heroin. The production pies *(left)* cover the percentages estimated to be manufactured by each country or region. The pies depicting U.S. supplies *(right)* illustrate only percentages that arrive in the United States. They do not include amounts used within source countries or regions, nor do they illustrate percentages that go to other parts of the world. Data taken from the *NNICC Report, 1985–1986* compiled by the U.S. Drug Enforcement Administration, Washington, D.C.

Long rows of plants lead to the horizon on a fully mechanized farm in northern Iran, where most of the nation's food is grown.

Agriculture

All but one-third of Iran is either mountains or desert. As a result, less than 10 percent of the country's total surface area is suitable for raising crops. Some people think that irrigation could triple this figure, but the amount of rain that falls in Iran could not replenish the water that would be tapped for crops. Water purification plants could remove the salt from the waters of the Persian Gulf for use in cities and factories. The cost of desalting water is high, however, and the government says it cannot afford to sponsor the project.

Farming without irrigation occurs in the north and northwest. In these regions there are many rivers and thousands of streams, so no water shortage exists. As a result, these areas produce enough food to feed one-third of the population.

Most of Iran's acreages grow wheat, barley, and rice. In addition to these main crops, farmers cultivate cotton, tobacco,

Sheep, goats, and cattle are raised throughout Iran but survive best where water supplies and grazing are plentiful.

59

Tea is among Iran's most important commercial crops and flourishes on large plantations. These workers are harvesting a crop in northern Iran.

sugar beets, dates, olives, corn, tea, and citrus fruits. Rice and tobacco grow primarily along the shores of the Caspian Sea. Olives, tea, medicinal herbs, and a variety of fruits and nuts are major commercial crops. Despite its output, however, Iran is not self-sufficient in food production.

Livestock raisers tend herds of sheep, goats, and cattle that total about 50 million head. Horses, camels, donkeys, and water buffalo work as beasts of burden and produce meat and milk.

Forestry and Fishing

Forests cover about one-third of the land, mostly near the Caspian Sea, and provide fuel and timber. Centuries of overcutting, however, have depleted many of the wooded areas. As a result, oil and natural gas are replacing charcoal as fuel. Iran's temperate-zone hardwoods include oak, beech, maple, Siberian elm, and walnut. Regions near the Zagros Mountains and in the provinces of Khorasan and Fars abound with pistachio, oak, maple, and walnut.

Fishing is a small but important industry that thrives especially along the Caspian Sea. Sturgeon, bream, whitefish, salmon, mullet, carp, catfish, perch, and roach are among the usual catches, and shrimp, sole, and tuna come from the Persian Gulf. Fishing is important both as a food source within Iran and as an export industry. For example, the eggs of sturgeon are made into a salty delicacy called caviar, and some varieties of Iranian caviar sell at high prices on the international market.

A catch of beluga sturgeon is laid out at a small dock in Enzeli along the Caspian Sea. The eggs of beluga are commonly used to make caviar, an expensive seafood delicacy.

Iranian fishermen arrange their nets to capture the day's haul of fish, which may include sturgeon, salmon, and perch.

Energy and Transportation

Thermal heating plants that burn petroleum, natural gas, and coal produce roughly 80 percent of Iran's energy. Almost all of the remaining energy is from hydroelectric facilities. Greater demands for electrical power within Iran—for both household and industrial needs—have increased the amount of oil used in the country. Of 1.2 billion barrels of oil produced per year in the 1980s, Iran itself consumed almost 300 million or about 25 percent annually. Among low-income groups, however, kerosene and wood remain the primary sources of fuel.

Iran possesses among the world's largest deposits of petroleum. Before Iraqi bombings damaged the refining facilities at Abadan and Bahtaran, these sites pro-

Independent Picture Service

As workers tar a new stretch of road, a rural Iranian relies on a more traditional form of transport.

Courtesy of Embassy of the Islamic Republic of Iran, Ottawa

This dam at Isfahan regulates the flow of the Zayandeh River in central Iran. Despite the country's oil reserves, hydroelectric power provides 20 percent of Iran's energy needs.

At the port of Bandar Abbas, which lies in the Strait of Hormuz, a cargo ship waits at the dock.

cessed about eight billion gallons of oil per year, most of which were exported to the Soviet Union.

Tehran is the hub of a system of roads that connects the city to the 24 provincial capitals in Iran. Two paved roads run across the country from Turkey to Afghanistan and from Iraq to Pakistan. In the 1980s vehicles drove along 15,000 miles of first-class and along 16,000 miles of second-class roads. Most Iranians travel in buses, which are modern and comfortable in urban areas. Animals and bicycles are common forms of transportation in rural areas.

Before the 1979 revolution, Tehran had a major air terminal serviced by more than a dozen international airlines. Iran Air, the national airline, continues to fly to several European cities, but it no longer flies to the United States because of discord between the two countries. The railway network, which has about 3,000 miles of track, connects Tehran to the gulf and to the Turkish border. In 1983 construction started on a line that would run from Kerman to Zahedan and would link up with the railroads of Pakistan.

Before the outbreak of the war with Iraq, Iran had several major ports on the Persian Gulf. Fighting destroyed parts of the oil terminals at Abadan and at Khark Island; Bandar Khomeini also lies near the area damaged by the war. The largest port, Bandar Abbas, is relatively safe, but it does not handle foreign trade.

The Future

Iran has experienced chaotic times in the last decade. Corruption marred the shah's rule, and his secret police inspired fear among the population. Furthermore, the shah created many enemies by pushing Iran into a program of widespread modernization. In 1979 a conservative, religious government replaced the Westernized approach of the former regime.

In the 1980s Iran's economy suffered greatly from lack of innovation and capital. The war with Iraq has consumed large quantities of money and has caused countless military and civilian casualties on both sides. Terrorist tactics that strike out mainly at Western nations have won the regime few friends internationally. Iran's oil and its revolutionary Islamic principles are exported with equal vigor. The advanced age of Ruhollah Khomeini has caused concern, and his successor will be important in determining the country's direction. If the government can become more stable, a better future may yet be possible for this strong Islamic nation.

63

Index